Liz's Lefse

By
Elizabeth Onstad Ellertson

Flower designs on cover and throughout the interior
courtesy of Obsidian Dawn: www.obsidiandawn.com

Liz's Lefse

Rivershore Books

My first introduction to lefse was with my Grandma.

I was born on a farm near Melvin, Minnesota in Polk County, township of Onstad, on February 3rd, 1927.

The house I was born in

The only baby picture I have of me

My parents were Emma Wilhelmina Wentzel Onstad and Iver Theadore Onstad.

My parents' wedding photo, May 6, 1926

They had been married nine months when I was born. My mom was 21 (would be 22 in May) at the time.

2

A painting of my grandparents (Wentzel)

I was the first of twelve children and was born at home. My Grandma Onstad, Embjor (Emma) Krogen Onstad, helped with my birth.

Grandma and Grandpa Onstad, 1947

Grandpa's first wife, Ingrid Christianson, and their oldest child, Esther, about eight years old, died in a flu (or diphtheria) epidemic in 1898. They had three other children: Paul, Anga, and Oliver.

3

He married my grandma in 1899. They had eight children together; one died at birth.

My dad, Iver, was the oldest, then Lars, Peter, Esther, Nordahl, Reuben, and Orville. Lars drowned when he was 16. My dad was a farmer but also had other jobs during the depression and after WWII.

Sadly, my mother did not get along with her in-laws, so I only came to know many of my cousins on my dad's side as adults and become good friends with them, making lefse with Barb and traveling to Jamaica with Barb and Uncle Nord and to Norway with Jeanne and Pete. On my mother's side, I met my uncles and aunts when I was young. After I retired, I did meet Aunt Alma when I was in Seattle and visited Aunt Martha in Devils Lake, ND, a few times. I met a couple cousins but never stayed in touch with any of them.

Peter was a pastor in Lutheran parishes in Minnesota and Iowa. He married Alice Olson in 1931 and they had two children, Peter and Jeanne. Alice died in 1946. In 1949, he married Jesse Hanson. After Jesse died, he married Olina Opsahl and they lived in Moorhead, MN. After he retired, he was a pastor in Oriska, ND, driving from Moorhead every Sunday. I, with Karen, Glen, and family, visited there once. Peter died in 1997 at 93. Olina lived to be 99. Pete and Marti live in Burnsville, MN, and Jeanne and Wayne Hole live in Fargo, ND.

Esther never married. She graduated from Concordia College then taught music at Detroit Lakes High School. I was living with my grandparents in Ada and going to high school at that time, and Esther would come home weekends and give me piano lessons and instructions to practice an hour a day all week. She taught in Oakridge, Tennessee, during the war and then taught at Luther College in Teaneck, New Jersey, for twenty-three years. She wrote a book called *Courage for Today and Hope for Tomorrow*, a study on Revelations. She taught voice lessons, directed choirs, taught Bible studies, and was a director at Camp Winnie. Starting in the 80s, she flew often to visit us and spent most Christmas Eves with our family, always insisting we pause our gift opening to watch the St. Olaf Christmas Concert. She traveled to many countries and lived many years in New Jersey, where I visited her often, including helping her move to Minneapolis when she was 89. She lived in Minneapolis, where I visited her nearly every week, and we brought her to our home for many holidays until she died at 99 years old. Her mind was sharp until the day she died.

Nordahl graduated from the University of Minnesota with a degree in electrical engineering. He worked for the government during the war. He was part of a research group that worked on the development of the C1 Bomber Autopilot. He also got an award for Civilian Service to the US Navy. He invented a way to make pellets out of taconite and got other awards. He married Millie, a widow with two small boys, Robert and Jack. Her first husband was killed in a plane accident during WWII. Together they had a daughter, Barbara. After Millie died, Barbara moved in with Nordahl, now 101, and they live in Edina.

Reuben also became an electrical engineer. He was in the Navy during the war. He married Gertrude and they had three children, Mark, Eric, and Juliana. Reuben and Gert live in San Diego, CA.

Orville was also in the Navy during the war. He married Verona Fetting, and they had three children, Alan, John, and Lisa. Orville lives in Ada, MN, where he and Verona both grew up. For many years, he worked for Schmitts Music in Fargo, tuning pianos. Verona died some years ago. When I was in school in Ada, Verona was in my class.

My mother never liked her in-laws and I don't know why. It could have had something to do with my parents moving from the farm before Alvin was born.

Maybe there was a disagreement with my grandpa and they had to move.

Mom holding Louise, Dad holding Doris
Margaret, Alvin, me (Age 5)

In 1942, when I was 15, Lydia, the eleventh child, was born. The other children, in order, were: Margaret, Alvin, Doris, Louise, Geraldine, David, Philip, Norman, Luther, Lydia, and Mary.

Doris, Margaret (Luther), me (Lydia), Alvin
Phillip, Gerri, Louise, David
Norman

That year, during the Second World War, my dad joined the Navy. He was 42, my mother was 37, and they had 11 kids! Mary was born 6 years after Lydia, after my dad returned from the Navy. While my dad was in the Service, my mother paid for the farm and bought another adjoining farm. She got a nice allotment for all the dependents my dad had when he was in the Navy.

We were always poor, and we moved a lot when I was young. It was during the Depression in the 30s, but I don't ever remember being hungry. We always had a big garden, and my mother canned many quarts of vegetables and fruit. And we ate a *lot* of oatmeal—many times for both breakfast and supper . . . maybe even for lunch! I won't eat oatmeal now.

I'm not fond of bread pudding, either. My mother made a lot of that. We might have had gravy on bread, too, which I also don't like. Grandma used to send us meatloaf and lefse in the mail, and that was a real treat!

7

We baked all our own bread. A lot, for that big family! If we ever had "store-bought" bread or cereal, it was a rare treat. Having Corn flakes was like getting candy—and that didn't happen often. Almost everything we ate came from the farm.

I don't recall a lot about when I was real young. I remember being sent to school when I was four or five and hiding and crying because I was afraid to go—so I didn't have to go at that time.

I also cut my foot bad enough around that time that I had to go to the doctor for stitches and had to stay in bed for a while. That was the only time I remember ever going to a doctor. I can remember going to a field and getting watermelon with my dad, and one time Alvin threw something down the outdoor toilet and my dad had to fish it out. I think it belonged to one of the other kids. Of the six oldest children, Alvin was the only boy, so he was pretty spoiled.

When I was about eight, Margaret, Alvin, and I went to Grandma and Grandpa Onstad's, and they took us to the doctor in Ada to get our tonsils out. I used to go to my grandparents' almost every summer when I was little, and I have happy memories of staying with Grandma and Grandpa.

Grandma and Grandpa, with all their grandchildren
I am third from the bottom, next to the railing (Age 12)

I never knew my mother's parents. Her dad died when she was young, and her mother died when I was a baby.

By the time I went to school, we were living in Fisher, MN, in a huge house that my mother's mother had built when she was a young widow. My mother saw her dad (my grandfather) and her oldest brother, Paul, drown in the flooded Red Lake River when she was eleven. She always had a paranoid fear of water, and when we did go in she was always there to watch. Her mother, my grandmother, was left to raise the other seven children. Paul was the oldest, then Martha, Emma, Arno, Ralph, Herbert, Alma, and Roland. We lived there about three or four years, and I did first and second grades in one year there. I must have known first grade studies, besides being so smart (ha-ha), and the teacher moved me to second grade. Both grades were in the same room.

I can remember going around selling bunches of radishes from the garden. One time our parents were gone, and we picked all the peonies and pulled up all the radishes and went around selling them door to door. We must have been trying to help make some money. I don't remember if we sold them all, but I'm sure we all got spanked by an angry mother. At that time, my dad worked on WPA, the Works Progress Administration. It was set up by the government to create jobs for men during the Depression in 1935. He worked building highways and I don't know what else. I also remember him selling Wearever Cookware. He would go door to door and demonstrate cooking: something like Tupperware Parties used to be. He took any job he could to support the family; there was no Welfare back then that I knew of . . .

I remember my 8th birthday in Fisher. My mother always made an angel food cake for every birthday, but that year no one even mentioned my birthday all day, and I was sure everyone forgot. Finally that night my mother gave me an organdy dress she had made, and she had baked an angel food cake. They hadn't forgotten after all! I never forgot how sad I was, thinking no one was going to remember my birthday.

When we lived in Fisher, we all got the measles and had to stay in bed in a dark room so we wouldn't hurt our eyes. Geraldine was born at home in Fisher. We were all sent to the neighbors and my dad delivered her, as he did most of the kids. I think my mother's uncle owned the house and asked us to move. He moved the house to his farm between Fisher and Crookston. The next house I remember was near Oklee, MN. David, the first boy born after one boy and five girls, was born there. "It's a boy baby!" we all yelled. For a long time we called him "Boy Baby." Philip was also born there. One time when we lived there, I got mad because I had to stay home with David, the baby. Before the rest of the family came home, I took him and hid in the woods. I got a whipping after that episode!

Since I was the oldest I always had to stay home with the younger ones and I resented it. I think my parents went to church. It was in Oklee that we got to go to *Snow White*, too, but in the middle of the movie my mother came and took me to stay home with the baby while they went somewhere. I don't know why they had to leave, but I never saw the whole movie until it came out on video, maybe in 1995! I remember seeing my dad cry when his Grandma Krogen died while we lived there. That was the only time I ever saw him cry.

When I was 12, my parents bought the farm at Clearbrook: 3 miles from Leonard and about 30 miles from Bemidji. This was not good farming land; heavily wooded. They had cows, pigs, chickens, horses, and geese. We always had fresh eggs and plenty of milk to drink. Norman, Luther, Lydia, and Mary were all born there.

I went to a one room country school during the 7th and 8th grades.

8th grade school photo

In 8th grade, my teacher was an 18-year-old man teaching his first year. I thought he was pretty young to be a teacher. My best friend was Devona Engdahl. I was the only 8th grader, and there were two boys in 7th grade. My sister Margaret (one year younger than me) and Devona were in 6th grade. We walked to school. It seemed like 5 miles, but I guess it was only about a mile. We would bring lunch from home, like soup or stew in jars, and the teacher would warm it up on the stove in a pan of water. The school didn't have running water; they had a pump outside. Engdahls lived on a farm a couple of miles from us. Sometimes I got to sleep over at their house.

At home we all slept upstairs in one big, unfinished room. The boys on one side, and the girls were on the other. When it would get so hot in the summer, we would take a blanket and lay outside to cool off. The mosquitoes would almost eat us alive! Sometimes we built a bonfire and made a "smudge" fire…made it real smoky to chase the mosquitoes away. I'm sure we talked and giggled half the night. We would play "pump, pump, pull away", hide and seek, and must have played other games during the day, when we weren't doing chores.

In the winter it was so cold you could see your breath in the upstairs of the house. There was no insulation up there—just bare rafters. Of course we never slept alone; always two or three to a bed. That helped keep us warm. Not so much fun when someone wet the bed, though! In the morning we would hurry down to dress by the wood heater in the living room.

The house had a living room/dining room, a tiny bedroom, and a small kitchen downstairs. My parents had the bedroom, which was only large enough for a double bed and a dresser. The basement was just a dugout with a dirt floor. In the fall they stored all the canned goods down there, and potatoes, carrots, onions, parsnips, turnips, and rutabagas for winter. They made pickles and sauerkraut in big crocks and stored them there, too. They would butcher a pig and can the meat. Most of the meat was kept for my dad.

We never had running water; we hauled the water from a pump by the barn and threw the "slop" (wastewater) down the hill by the house. We always had a big pail in the kitchen for the "slop" water. Guess what we called it! A "slop pail"! Our toilet was an outhouse, and we took baths in a washtub when we were small. When we were older we took sponge baths in the kitchen with a basin of water. I remember Saturdays in the summer we would all get our hair washed. My mother would set up an assembly line of pans outside and first one would wash, then the next one (same water). Then we'd go to the next pan and rinse. I think there were three pans for rinsing. The last one had vinegar in the water, to get all the soap out. I don't remember if we washed in any order. Since I was the oldest I should have been first, right?

We hauled all the water for washing clothes, too. We would heat it in a copper boiler on the wood cook stove. We had two big cream cans by the stove for water and a reservoir on the stove. We always had a pail of water with a dipper for drinking. Everyone drank out of the same dipper. The washer was a

Maytag, with wringers and a gas motor. We had two tubs to rinse the clothes in. We rinsed them by hand and put them through the wringer. All the clothes were hung outside, even in the winter when we would bring them in after a while, to finish drying inside. The long underwear must have been quite a sight—frozen solid! All the water we used came from a hand-operated pump by the barn. We had a homemade cart with wheels to haul it from the barn to the house.

We also had homemade sleds, and I remember making ragdolls for the smaller kids for Christmas. I think all our toys were homemade. I got my only "store bought" doll when I was 12. I don't think I ever really played with it. I kept it in the box and took it out and looked at it. When I went to Ada, my mother let the smaller kids play with it—and it got wrecked.

All our clothes were handed down from cousins, and my mother sewed a lot. I got my first "store bought" outfit when I was 17 and went to Crookston to school. It was a brown suit, a skirt, and jacket. Girls didn't wear slacks or jeans in those days. We got one pair of shoes a year, for school in the fall. Summers we went barefoot most of the time.

When my dad was in the service, I had to help my brother Alvin (we called him Buddy) milk the cows, make hay in the summer, and cut pulp wood in the winter.

I always loved reading—still do!

We never had a tractor when I lived at home. We had a team of horses that did all the work of pulling the plow, mower, hay rake, cultivator, etc. I don't remember hitching up the horses, but I must have helped Alvin with that. I do remember driving them behind the hay rake. Sometimes we would ride the horses bareback. They were big work horses. In the summer we would make the hay. I threw a *lot* of hay on a hay rack and hauled and stacked it with Alvin. It was hot, dirty work, and we often took a break in a small creek to cool off.

We also had cows to milk...by hand. We had maybe eight cows, and Alvin and I milked them all. I always got the one who kicked! We had to tie her back legs together so she wouldn't hurt us. We did have some fun squirting milk at each other! Then we brought the milk into the house and put it in the separator to separate the cream from the skim milk. We sold most of the cream and drank skim milk. Once in a great while we could make butter. We would shake it in an old half gallon tin syrup pail. That was a treat! I remember putting lard and salt on our bread. *Yuck!*

Sometimes we had homemade ice cream—*that* was good!

We never had electricity when I was at home. We didn't have a refrigerator or even an icebox. We would put the milk in a cream can and lower it into an open well to keep it cool. We had dim kerosene lamps, but we had one Aladdin lamp that was very bright. I think the Aladdin was an expensive lamp, as I only remember having one. We had a radio that ran on a battery but could only listen to "The Old Fashioned Revival Hour." Once in a while if my parents were gone we'd listen to something like The Lone Ranger or Amos and Andy. I don't recall ever getting caught so we must not have run the battery down!

We heated with a wood space heater in the living room, and cooked on a wood stove in the kitchen. I remember sitting up all night when we canned corn, watching the pressure cooker and keeping the fire going. My mother used to can about 1,000 quarts of vegetables and fruit every year. When I was a teen she would have us push a table up to the bedroom door (she was in bed) and tell me how to can. We had a huge garden, which all of us had to help weed. We used to pull up radishes and carrots, wipe them off on our clothes, and eat them right out of the garden. A lot of the fruit that was canned grew wild, like juneberries, raspberries, plums, and strawberries. There were also chokecherries and other berries for jelly. We used to pick wild strawberries—each of us with a tin cup—and they were so small. My mother would mix them with rhubarb for sauce. Of course we ate a lot too, so it took a while to get a cup full.

When I was older, I used to help cut wood and even split it.

I also killed many chickens by chopping their heads off with an axe on the wood chopping block. We'd throw them on the ground until they quit flopping around. After that, we scalded them with boiling water and pulled the feathers off and then cut them open and pulled out the insides. (My grandson Jaymes calls them "guts.")

When I was 13, I went to stay with my grandparents in Ada, to go to high school. I went to and was confirmed in the Lutheran church there, and my cousin Russell was confirmed at the same. His dad was Oliver, and they also lived in Ada. Grandpa was the Superintendent of the Sunday School, and was active in the church. I remember Grandma going to "Ladies' Aid." I taught Sunday School some, too, and sang in the church choir. I also sang in the high school choir. Sometimes I baby sat for the church pastor and got 25 cents for the evening. I remember visiting Aunt Anga and Uncle Jarl and their four girls. Barbara, Ruth, and Mildred were older than me; Joyce was a little younger and closer to my age. They also lived in Ada, were a nice family, and I have happy memories of visiting them.

Aunt Esther was teaching in Detroit Lakes at that time, and came home on weekends. She gave me piano lessons and I had to practice an hour a day every week. She tried to get me interested in classical music but I wasn't too receptive to that! Every Saturday she would have this music on the radio—opera, I think—and explain it to me. I didn't like it at all! I guess I've always been a "country girl"!

Grandpa, Esther, and Grandma

17

I remember my grandpa sitting up close to the floor model radio listening to the news. And I remember when Pearl Harbor was bombed, probably how horrified everyone was.

My best friend in Ada was Margie Smith. She lived near my grandparents with her Grandma.

Me and Margie

We would walk to high school, which was through a park and across town. She had an older brother who had a car, a coupe. Once we got to ride in the rumble seat. That was fun! That was a seat that was in the back of the car where the trunk is, and it opened the opposite way that the trunk does, and there was a seat back there. Air conditioned, too! Just like a convertible! Another friend and neighbor was Pearle Gunderson. She was under 5 feet tall. And I was tall, almost 5'8", and skinny. I was the tallest one in my class in Ada, and felt like an awkward giant! My time in Ada was a happy time. My grandmother was a wonderful person and I felt she really loved me. I felt Grandpa did too but he was more reserved.

When the Second World War started, my dad went into the Navy.

Mama and Daddy

At that time there were eleven kids. I was the oldest at 15, and Lydia was the baby. My mother kept me out of school for two years, to help on the farm. She wouldn't let me go to back to Ada or to Clearbrook High School; she didn't think Clearbrook was a good enough school. At first I wrote to Margie but my mother opened my mail so I quit writing to anyone. Alvin, Margaret and I did most of the outside work during the next two years. We made pulp wood in the winter using a two man saw.

Pulpwood we cut and hauled to the yard to be sold

We cut the trees down, cut off the branches, cut them up into logs, and hauled them up to the farmyard and stacked them. We hauled them on a sled that the horses pulled. Then we sold the pulp wood. Because of this, Bill Olson used to call me a "stump jumper"!

When I was seventeen and Margaret 16, we were enrolled in the A.C. (Agricultural College) at Crookston. At that time, it was a high school for farm kids. Now it is the U of M Crookston. We lived right on the campus and the school year was only six months long: from October 1st to April 1st, so the kids could be home on the farm to help with planting in the spring and harvesting in the fall. I met Lorraine at school there. She was from a farm near Thief River Falls. I sang in the choir, too. We used to walk into Crookston when we had time off. I went there the year I turned 18. I thought I was too old to continue going to school, so I got a job when school was out. During the school year, Lorraine had stayed with a couple and watched their baby and worked for her room and board instead of living at the school. After school was out, she went home to the farm and I took her job. I helped with the housework and babysat. My mother was not happy about that at all! She tried to get me to come home, but I wouldn't. I wanted to be on my own and independent. I never lived at home after I was 18.

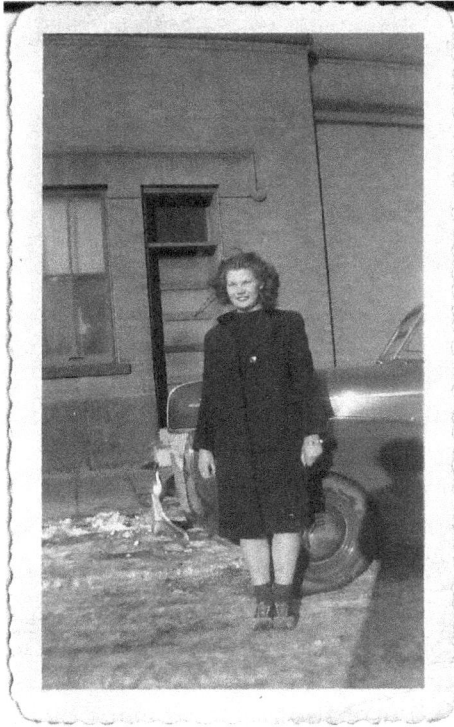

Me in Crookston, after I left school (Age 18)

Grand Forks

Then I went to work at the hospital in Crookston as a nurse's aide. I was going to join the Army Nurse Corps and become a nurse. Then the war was over and they didn't take any more in the Nurse Corps.

In the fall, I quit that job and went picking potatoes in North Dakota near Grand Forks. That was hard work, and I never did it again!

The day the war was over, everyone in town was out in the streets, yelling and cheering; so glad it was finally over and the service men could come home. Soon, my dad was home, too. He was never sent out of the states—because of his large family, I suppose. He was stationed at Farragut, Idaho, Coeur d' Alene, Idaho, and San Diego, California.

For a while I was a waitress in the hotel, still in Crookston. Then, when I was 19 or 20, I came to the Cities. Lorraine was already in Minneapolis. I came

22

with another friend from Crookston, but she hated the Cities and only stayed a week. Lorraine and I roomed together.

My first job was at Woolworth's downtown, squeezing oranges in an orange juice booth. That didn't last long; very boring! I got a job as a waitress/fry cook in Ray & Arne's Hamburger Shop on Lake Street. Lorraine was already working there. It was a small place with 6 or 8 booths and a counter. All the neighborhood workers stopped in for coffee, breakfast, lunch, etc. We all got to know the milkmen, the theater operator, and the store owners. We lived about ten blocks away, on 26th and Harriet, and I walked to work. I worked there off and on for the next four years or so. Every time I left town and came back I always had a job there. I think I was a pretty good waitress...the customers used to call me the "Lake Street Flash." It wasn't too easy; we had to be a fry cook and dishwasher, too. You had to be quick!

One time my friend Karna and I were going to California. We only got as far as Great Falls, Montana, and we were broke. I don't remember why we were traveling that route. So we got a job on a Dude Ranch in the Rocky Mountains. It was way up: 20 miles by either boat or horseback after leaving the road. We went by boat. We were only there two weeks, until the previously hired help came. It was beautiful up there. They had a warm spring pool. It was cool, but the pool was warm. We cleaned cabins and got things ready for the tourists. It was so cool at night we had a fire in the stove and blankets, and it was June. When we left there and went down from the mountains, it was 90 degrees in Great Falls. And we were wearing sweaters! We never did get to California, and instead came back to Minneapolis.

Karna and me, hitchhiking!

Another time Karna and I were again going to California, and we stopped in Cheyenne, Wyoming, where I had two uncles, my mother's brothers, Ralph and Herbert Wentzel, and their wives. I think they worked at the air base there, or were in the Air Corps. From there we went to Denver, Colorado, and needed money so tried to get a job. There were no jobs in Denver, so we went back to Cheyenne. Both of us got jobs doing housework.

I worked for a young widow with two kids. She treated me like one of the family. She was from Grand Forks and had gone to school with my cousin, Elizabeth Onstad (Paul Onstad's daughter). I worked there six months, spending my 21st birthday out there. And once again, we came back to Minneapolis. Back to the same house to live in and the same job at the hamburger shop. By this time, Ray & Arne had sold the shop to Betty and Al Sand, and they changed the name to Betty & Al's. One time Grandma and Orville came to the restaurant while I was working. Betty and Al were Polish and dark haired. Grandma said: "Elisabet, are they Catolic?" and when I said yes she said I better get another job. I guess the best people were Norwegian Lutherans!

My landlady, Bernice Walker, (Catholic also) was like a mother to me, and if they didn't have a room to rent I stayed right with them in the lower part of the duplex. One time I helped them remove all the wallpaper in the whole lower floor, so they could paint the walls. Bernice and her husband Charles had three girls and one son.

Soon, Karna and I decided we wanted to get an apartment of our own. At the Walker's we only had a sleeping room. So we moved near downtown Minneapolis, on 15th and Nicollet. I still worked at Betty & Al's and walked to work. Our apartment had four rooms, a kitchen, living room, and two bedrooms. In the kitchen we had an icebox. No refrigerator. The ice was delivered in large blocks and put in the top part of the icebox to keep the food cool. If we forgot to empty the pan underneath where the water drained from the melting ice, we had a flooded kitchen—and that happened more than once!

Then Karna moved to Montana and her younger sister, Ruby, moved in with me. She had just graduated from high school and moved to the Cities from near Willmar and got a job. She met Gene Hartman and started going out with him.

Back at the hamburger shop, I met Harvey Burgess and fell madly in love. I went with him for a year, and we were married in April of 1949.

We were married by a minister in his home, with just two friends as our witnesses. Our first apartment was on James Ave. South, near Lake Calhoun. I think we had two rooms and shared the kitchen and bath. Ruby moved with us for a few months. We had the bedroom and she slept on the couch. Pretty cozy for newlyweds! Not too long after we were married, Ruby and Gene were married, too.

Harvey and me

Soon we moved into one room that had a bed, table, two chairs, refrigerator, and a two-burner hot plate to cook on and shared the bath with the other renters. He went to school and I worked (still at Betty & Al's). At this house I met Myrt and Lois Tolzman from near Amery, WI. They had the housekeeping room next to us. We lived there until I had to quit working, when I was six or seven months pregnant with Ginny. They didn't allow women to work when they started to "show."

We moved in with Harvey's mother. After he finished school he didn't work much, so we had no money. He went to Auto Body School, but never worked long at a job.

Our car

He had many jobs during the three years we were married, but didn't keep any of them. His brothers Jerry, Murray, and Norman were at home, too. Then Janette moved home also, and started going with Ernie.

In September of 1950, Ginny was born.

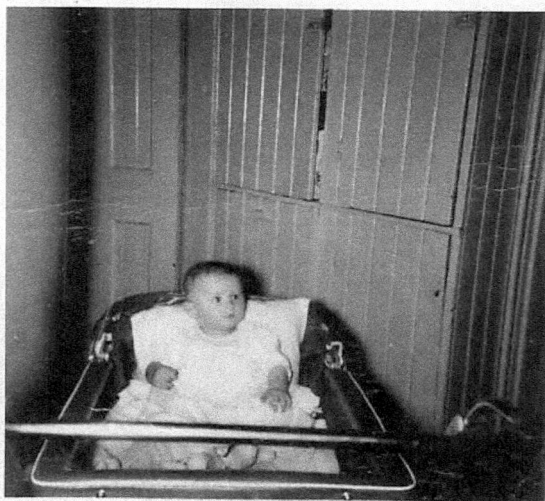

My daughter Virginia (Ginny)

I went back to work at the hamburger shop when Ginny was five weeks old and Harvey's mom stayed home to babysit. She had been cleaning houses for people. That lasted six months; until Ginny would go to her and not me...she thought I was a stranger. So we moved into a two room/share the bath place. By this time, Lorraine was married and had two girls, and she babysat for me. I would push Ginny in a stroller to their house on my way to work every morning.

Soon, Lorraine and John bought some land out in the country, in Blaine, and built a house. We used to drive out to see them and stay overnight. It seemed like a long way at the time, but was not far from where I live now! Highway 65 was a two lane road, and there were no freeways anywhere.

My marriage to Harvey was not a very good marriage, as he didn't work and had many girlfriends in the three years we were married. Then he started working at the Twin City Arsenal, and in September when Ginny was one year old, I started there too. He met Ruby (not the Ruby I had lived with) out there, left on New Year's Day 1952, and Ginny and I moved back in the same house I had lived in before I was married. The third floor apartment was vacant. I got a roommate who had a boy ten months old. I worked nights and babysat during the day, and the other girl worked days, so neither of us had to pay a babysitter. That lasted for about three months, and the landlady kicked her out. Then I moved to the second floor, and Janette moved in with us. She worked days and watched Ginny at night, while I worked the night shift. By this time, we had the whole second floor of the duplex. For a time, we had another girl with her little girl living there too. We had three bedrooms, a living room, dining room, bath, and screened in porch: plenty of room. The Walker's three girls used to fight over who was going to come up and help us with dishes. I know they wanted to play with Ginny!

In 1953, Myrt introduced me to Verlyn. I liked him at first sight. I thought he had the most beautiful eyes! And he was so good to his mom. He used to take Ginny and I both out for Sunday dinner.

Me and Verlyn, 1953

    We were married in September, 1953, four days after Ginny's third birthday. Janette and Ernie were our witnesses. We were married in Duluth by a Judge. Ruby and Gene took care of Ginny while we were gone. On our way home from Duluth, we stopped in Amery to see Grandma Ellertson. She loved Ginny right away and told Verlyn: "Now you have to adopt this little girl." What a wonderful lady she was!

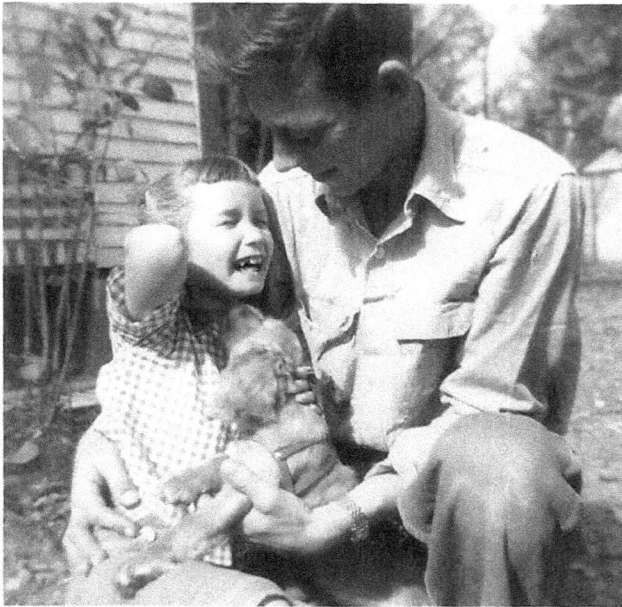

Verlyn with Ginny

Soon, Verlyn adopted Ginny. We bought a 27 foot trailer from Dorothy and Roy in a park in Roseville. They had lived in it for four years and had three girls: Mary, Barb, and Kathi. The trailer had a toilet, but we had to walk to the main building to shower (about a block). I gave Ginny baths in the kitchen sink. We bought a roll-away for Ginny to sleep on in the tiny bedroom, and we slept on a hide-a-bed in the tiny living room.

I worked at the Arsenal for six months after we married, until they closed and I was laid off. I then got a job in Roseville as a fry cook, working nights, and Verlyn watched Ginny and worked days at Purina. He went to school while we lived there and got a maintenance job at Purina. Every weekend we drove

31

out to Amery to his mom's. In 1955, we bought our first new car: an Oldsmobile 88. Blue, of course! The total cost was $2,000!

We lived there for four years until Karen was born. A 27 foot trailer just wasn't big enough for all of us!

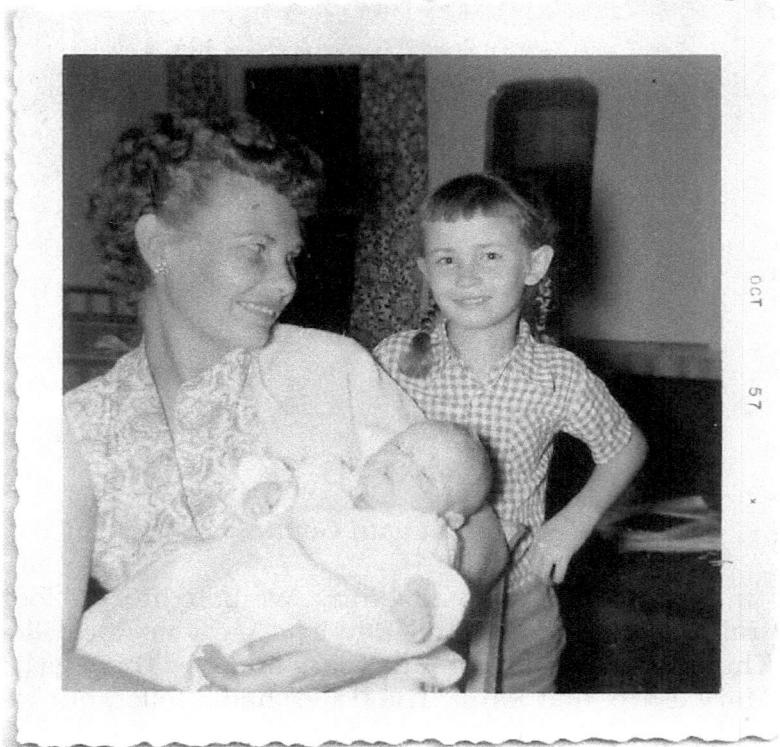

Me and my daughters, Ginny and Karen

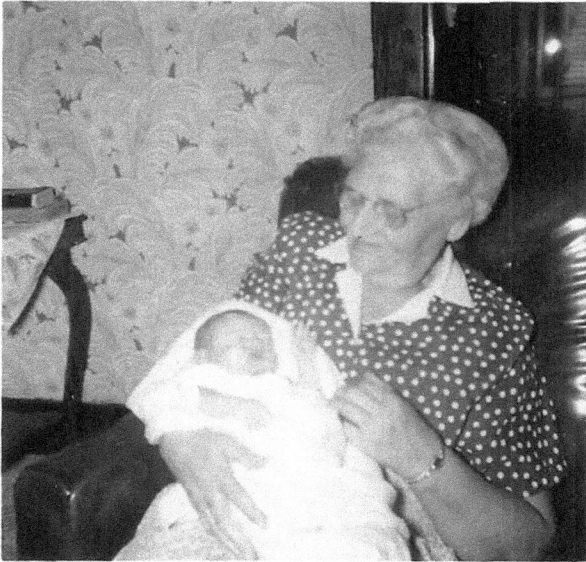

Grandma Ellertson with Karen

After Karen was born, we put Ginny's doll buggy next to our hide-a-bed for her to sleep in. It was just a bit crowded! Now motor homes are larger than what we lived in for four years. A few years ago, I found out that my friend Lyla and her husband lived in the same trailer court at the same time Dorothy and Roy did.

So at the end of August, 1957, when Karen was two weeks old, we bought a one room, furnished cabin with a porch at Coon Lake Beach, pulled the trailer out, and moved into the cabin. When we moved we had a new car, a boat and motor, and two kids.

The cabin

Verlyn enclosed the porch for a bedroom for the girls, and we moved our hide-a-bed in from the trailer. We had an oil space heater, no bathroom (outdoor potty), and a hand pump by the sink. I pumped all the water for washing clothes and everything. We ran a hose out from the sink for the wastewater, and let it run out on the ground. The first few weeks I washed clothes by hand, with a washboard until my knuckles bled. Stupid!! I could have gone to a Laundromat in Forest Lake. Maybe not, with a two week old baby! Then we got an Easy Spin Dry washer. This machine had two tubs, a washer and attached next to it was a spinner you lifted the washed clothes into and they spun all the water out. I think I still had to rinse the clothes and spin them again. I still had to heat all the water on the stove after I pumped it by hand. Ginny would have her bath in a wash tub and I had a baby bath tub for Karen.

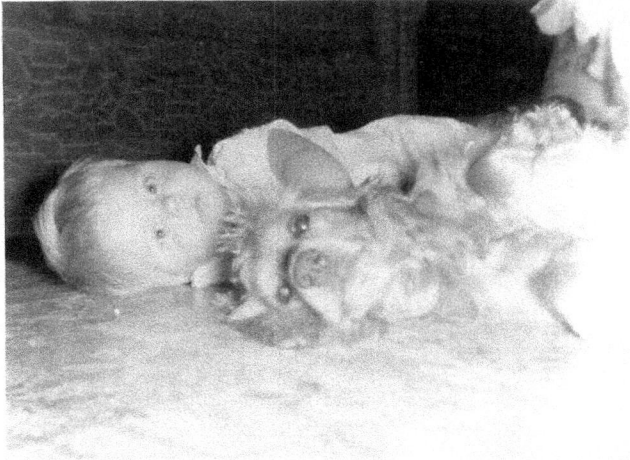

Karen and our dog Pixie

We loved living at the lake. Whenever we could, we were down at our dock. That year Karen and I spent a lot of time in the sun. She was "brown as a berry!" We met Verna and Bill, who became our closest friends. We also met Allens, Schmidts, Bensons, and more at the beach. The ladies had a card club, and we met once a week—mostly to talk.

The next spring we started building. We turned the cabin around and had the basement dug. Verlyn laid the blocks and I mixed cement and carried blocks to him. When we had the basement ready, we got an electric pump! That was our Christmas present that year. The next spring we added on the two bedrooms and a bath. We put the new roof on over Memorial Day, and it rained all weekend! We had moved a lot into the basement and covered the rest. We took most of our clothes and Ginny and Karen to Jhordis and Herman's for the weekend. Jhordis was Verlyn's sister, and they lived on a farm near St. Croix Falls, WI.

A year or so later, we added on to the kitchen, making it larger. Norman and Philip helped put the roof on at that time.

Building!

Verlyn on the roof

The house in progress

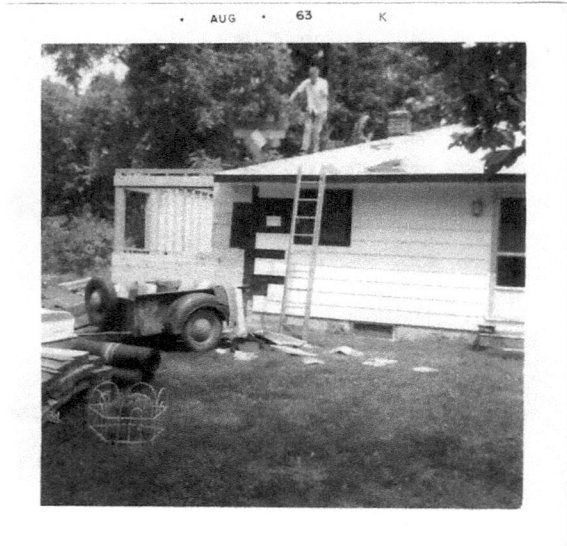

Norman and Phillip helping with the addition

The finished house!

That summer I finally learned to water ski. It took me all summer to get up enough nerve to stand up on the skis. I must have been a sight, riding around the lake on water skis, squatting down! I never learned to swim, so I was cautious—but I had the best life jacket money could buy!

Our boat

When Karen was 18 months old, I went to work at McMillan's in St Paul. There were six of us from the Coon Lake area working there, and we took turns driving. Katie Campbell was working there when I started. It was a good place to work. I worked mostly in the press room, where we had to lift scoop shovels full of steel cases into a hopper from a big bin. I worked there seven years. Then at the Arsenal, inspecting bullets, when they reopened, for another seven years, and finally to Medtronic in 1973. Medtronic at that time was on a four day work week, nine and a half hours a day. It was like having a vacation every week! Every Friday Verna and I would go to garage sales, the bank, and out to lunch. I felt really fortunate to get in there, and enjoyed my job there in packaging.

Karen and Ginny, enjoying the snow

When Karen was about three and four Grandma Ellertson lived with us two winters and babysat and cooked. What a treat, to come home after work and have supper ready! One thing, Verlyn had gotten a deer and we had the meat in the freezer and guess what Grandma fixed nearly every night? Venison! After that when we got a deer we had it made into smoked sausage and lunch meat, mixed with beef. Much better! When Grandma was with us she also made lefse and tried to teach me. I didn't learn much, it was much easier letting her do it. Years later when Grandma went into a nursing home I had to learn; no one else in the family made it. She gave me a recipe, so much of this, so much of that, not measuring, so it was pretty much learn-by-doing. I had a lot of messes but I didn't give up and even Grandma approved of my lefse when I would bring her some in the nursing home. I have used a hundred pounds of potatoes or more every year making lefse and giving it all away. Now Jaymes and Jansina can make it so they will keep up the tradition.

During these years, we bought two houses at Coon Lake Beach to rent out. We had to clean, clean, clean, and remodel, remodel, remodel, before we rented them out. It was quite a job, besides working full time and doing the cleaning, washing, cooking, etc. at home. Then we bought an old building in Minneapolis, and remodeled that into four apartments. By the time we finished that, I was so sick of cleaning up other peoples' dirt I didn't care if I ever saw another rental property.

Our first motorhome

41

We had two different motor homes these years. We traveled mostly up to a lake in the summer. One year we went to California, to Bjarne and Alice's. Another time we went to the Black Hills in South Dakota, and Medora in North Dakota. We finally sold it, because we didn't use it enough. We went up to Mizpah every fall when the guys went deer hunting. Olsons had a house up there. I always took a week's vacation during deer hunting season. Verna, Jo Ann, and I would do the cooking when the guys went hunting. We went up there some summers, too.

Ginny and Denny's wedding

In May of 1970 Ginny and Denny married. On December 26, 1970, I became a grandmother for the first time when Randy was born to Ginny and Denny.

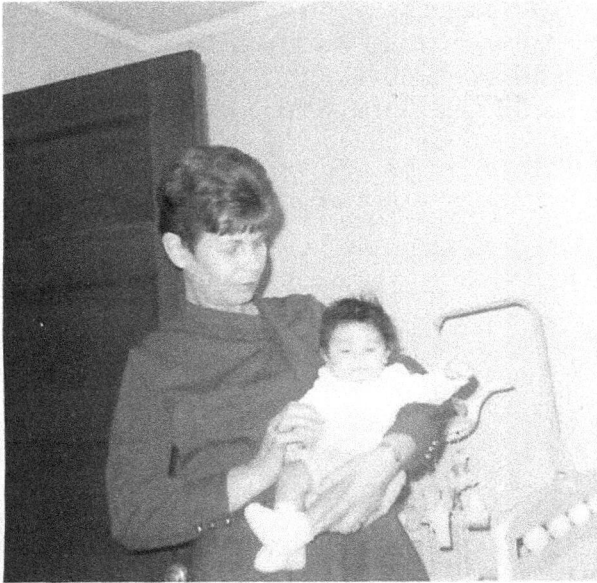

Randy's baptism

They lived in Minneapolis at that time, then moved to Coon Rapids, and finally bought a house in Elk River when Randy was about seven. They divorced in 1987 and Ginny lived there alone until she sold the house and moved to Webster, WI.

In 1975 my sister Louise died in a car accident on her way home to New Mexico, after visiting my parents on the farm. Her three children were with her and were injured. I went to the funeral in Continental Divide, NM. This was my first time on a plane. I flew to Albuquerque, NM., and changed planes in Denver, CO. Denny's parents lived in Albuquerque and they picked me up at the airport. Alvin and Marilynn drove from Texas and I rode with them to Cont. Divide, about 100 miles.

In 1979, Karen and I went to Norway with Marie Krogen. We were backpacking and had planned a month-long trip throughout Europe, England, and Norway. Marie was going to spend the month with her sister in Norway while Karen and I traveled, and we would spend the last week in Norway with her. On our second day in Oslo, I fell and broke my ankle, ruining our trip.

Karen pushing my wheelchair in Norway

I spent four days in the hospital, a few days in a YWCA kind of place, before we got a flight home. When I left the hospital they gave me crutches and let us borrow a wheelchair. So Karen took me all over Oslo, even a trip on the Oslo Fjord! Since we would be going home, we bought down comforters, Norwegian sweaters, jewelry, and Karen ordered mugs with our names on them. Karen also bought her baby buggy there. We had everything but the buggy shipped home. We must have been quite a sight coming home with me in a wheelchair! Lucky for us I had taken out trip insurance, which paid for everything, and I was put on medical at work with full pay. It was an unforgettable experience!

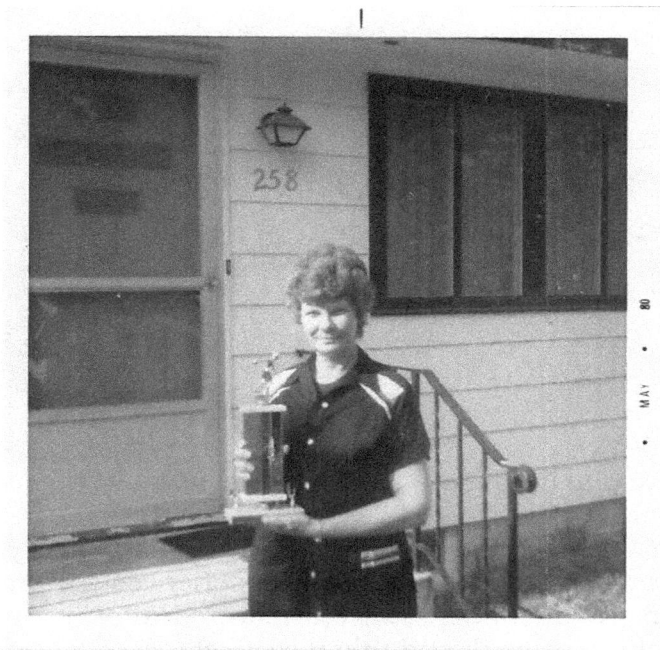

1980: I won a bowling trophy!

In 1982, Verlyn and I divorced. I lived alone at Coon Lake until 1984, when I sold the house and moved to Blaine. I bought a quad home and was very happy there. I loved the location: close to work, Northtown, the doctor, and I had many friends close by. And I didn't have to worry about any outside work like mowing the lawn or blowing snow.

Making lefse was—and is—a regular occurrence

In January and February of 1984, I had aneurysms operated on in my head. I truly experienced a "miracle" when the aneurysms were discovered after a routine eye check at work and taken care of!

After my divorce, I started traveling. My first trip in 1982 was to Lake Tahoe with Lyla, Doris, (from work) Betty, and Ellsworth. They had planned the trip for a while and asked me along when they heard that Verlyn had left. Lyla, Doris, and I stayed three to a room. It was a fun trip. We flew into Reno and rented a car there for the drive to Tahoe. My next trip was to the World's Fair in Knoxville, TN. In the fall of 1982, I was with "Chopper," a girl I bowled with. There were five of us in a big fancy van. I even drove it through Chicago! We had a great time.

After putting herself through college, Karen was teaching school in Thief River Falls when she met Glen.

Karen and Glen's wedding

They were married on June 8th, 1985, on her Onstad great grandparents wedding anniversary.

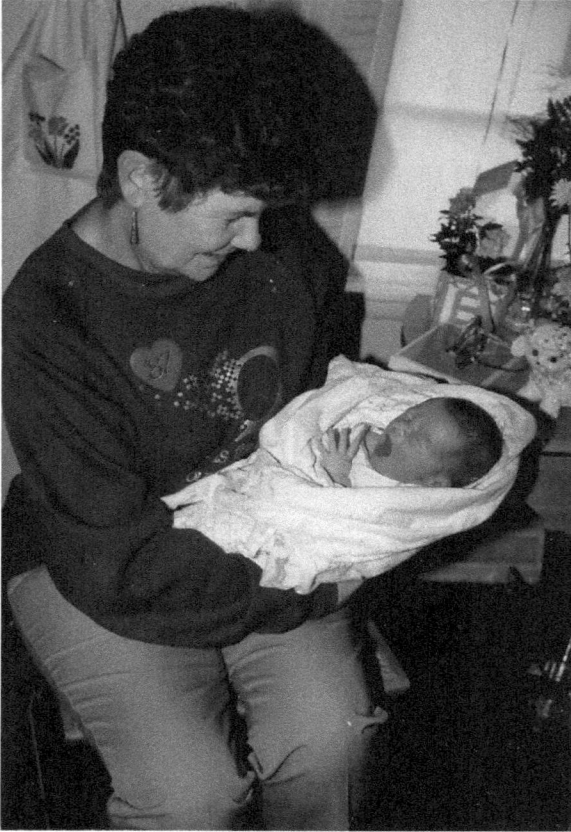

Jaymes with "Grandma Liz" (me)

They bought a house in Moorhead and on October 15, 1987, I became a grandma for the second time when Jaymeson was born and a third time on September 18, 1989 when my favorite granddaughter, and Jaymes' favorite sister, Jansina Elizabeth, was born.

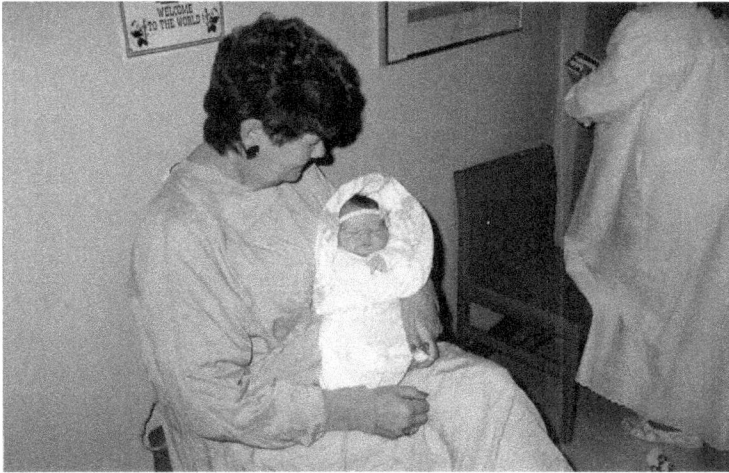

Me holding Jansina

I made many trips to Moorhead when they lived there, especially after my retirement.

During one of these years my siblings had a family reunion at Alvin's in Texas. I drove down by myself and stayed with my favorite sister-in-law on the Onstad side, Marilynn, Alvin's ex-wife.

Texas reunion

When I got to Dallas, I took the wrong direction on the freeway. After miles and miles (it felt like), I finally saw a McDonalds and pulled off to call. I knew Marilynn was working so I called Carla. She was at work, but David was home and he came and led me to their house. I had pulled off just a few blocks from their house! All my siblings except Doris, Margaret, and Luther were there, and it was a nice reunion.

My retirement party at Medtronic

I retired in 1990, and spent two weeks in New Jersey with Aunt Esther, packing her things so they could remodel her apartment. I flew out there, then we drove Esther's car back to Minnesota. When her apartment was ready we drove back to New Jersey, and after helping her unpack I flew home. This was a trying time; Esther was not the easiest person to get along with.

By the twin towers, 1993

She drove into New York City and I got to go to the top of the World Trade Center, the United Nations building, Wall Street, churches, and more. One day we took a boat from the Jersey side and went to the Statue of Liberty and Ellis Island. She did do a good job of showing me around.

Gerri and I

That same year I flew to Seattle and spent two weeks with my sister Gerri. One day she let me take her car and I drove downtown, to the wharf and around town. Another time with her car I drove to Squim, where friends from Minnesota had moved, and visited them.

At the Hershey's museum in PA

One year when Glen was in Massachusetts for his job, Karen, Jaymes, Jansina, and I drove out there. We went to the Amish in PA, saw the Liberty Bell and Betsy Ross house in Philadelphia, Washington, DC, New York City with Esther, a ride in Central Park, rode the Staten Island Ferry, then to Mass. With Glen on the weekend we saw Boston, the Mayflower, Ocean Spray Cranberry Museum, and more.

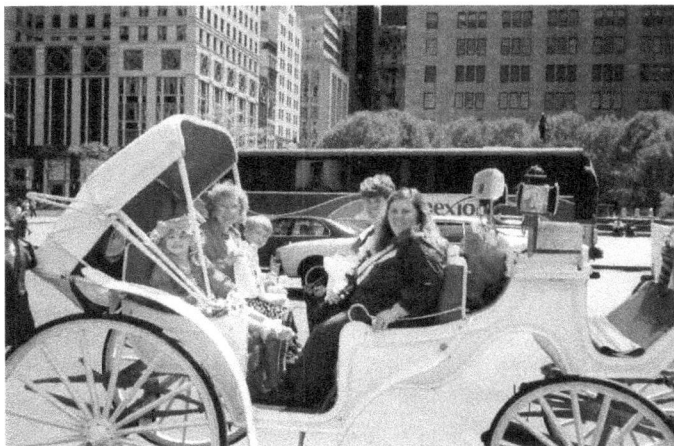

Carriage ride in Central Park

I started traveling more after I retired. In 1997, Karen and her family moved to Buffalo, New York. I drove out there four times while they lived there and got to see Niagara Falls, Toronto, Canada, Corning, New York, the factory there, parks, and more. We stopped in Olean, NY, at the Cutco factory, but they don't do tours. It was at this time that I got to know Norm and Wanda and Phil and Pat better, and they would be my stopping off place on my trips back from NY.

Florida with Betty, Lyla, and Betty, 1988

After I was divorced, I went on many trips, many with my friend Lyla. We went to the Virgin Islands, Scandinavia, Dominican Republic, the Bahamas, Mexico, Reno, Nevada, a Cruise, and many trips to Las Vegas.

My traveling buddies and good friends, Verna and Bill

After my retirement I started traveling with Verna and Bill in their motorhome. I was so fortunate they asked me along. We went out East once, west to Montana, the Canadian Rockies, and Lake Louise, south to Florida, Texas, Arizona, Las Vegas, and places in between!

I found a dance partner!

Relaxing during one of our many trips

I think we never missed an Outlet Mall wherever we were! We would buy Christmas and birthday gifts for the whole year. And sometimes we would get to a garage sale or two. We always had such a great time and got along so well. We went to the Hostfest in Minot, ND a few times too, as did Al and Jo Ann. When I ate rumagrot Al and Bill called it wallpaper paste. But we all liked lutefisk and they served it at Hostfest every day! How blessed I was to have them for friends!

In 2009 Verna passed away and I still miss her so much. Both Jo Ann and Al died before her.

I visited Disney World with my grandchildren multiple times

In 1998 I went on a two week trip to Norway with Cousin Jeanne, her daughter Jennifer, Cousin Pete, his daughter Alyson and son Greg. We had a small bus and own driver, Raymond. We traveled from Oslo to Bergen and back to Oslo. We stopped in Lillehammer, had a trip on the Geiranger Fjord, other fjords, saw Folk Museums, took the cable car in Bergen to the top of Mt. Ulriken and much much more. In Sjkak we met cousin Lars, his wife, Embjorg and son Oddbjorn. They took us to the Aanstad farm where Grandpa Onstad was born. It was a wonderful and unforgettable trip!

A trip with family to Norway

In 2001 Karen, Glen, Jaymes, and Jansina moved back from Buffalo and bought a house in Blaine one mile from my townhouse. They had a lot of work to do on it and squeezed in with me for a few months while they remodeled, or built, getting it livable. They put their queen mattress on my double futon in the spare bedroom, Jansina slept with me, and poor Jaymes had the couch in the living room. They had a lot of work to do and continued to do it after they moved in. Now they have a beautiful home. It's been great having them so close!

Shortly after Karen and Glen moved back Esther moved back to MN and bought a condo in Golden Valley. We saw a lot of her and she spent lots of Thanksgivings and nearly every Christmas Eve with us. She passed away in 2009, just days after her 99th birthday.

When Jaymes graduated from Anoka Ramsey, Jaymes, Jansina, and I drove to Dallas and stayed with Carla and family. On our way home we detoured to San Antonio and stayed there two days, and also stopped in Oklahoma City.

Our trip to Texas

Family in Texas

In 2007 Karen and Glen hosted an Onstad Family reunion at their home. It was a great success and well attended.

2007 Family Reunion

Family Reunion: Siblings

It was great to see my siblings, in-laws, nieces, nephews and cousins. And even two uncles, Nord from Edina, Orville from Ada and also Aunt Esther! They came from California, Texas, Illinois, North Dakota, Washington and Minnesota. Doris, Lydia and Alvin did not attend.

Uncles Nord and Orville, and Aunt Esther

In 2008 I sold my townhouse and moved to the Cottages of Spring Lake Park. I love it here and as I am renting I don't have to worry about any upkeep anymore.

Outside of my Cottage

In 2009 I traveled to Jamaica with Uncle Nord and Barb for a two week stay in their Villa in the hills of Jamaica. Beautiful and the weather was perfect! It was fun visiting with them and meeting Jamaicans they knew and seeing other parts of Jamaica.

In November 2010 I had a cancerous kidney removed at the Mayo Clinic. It was found when my heart doctor did an ultrasound before putting a stent in an artery. I was scheduled to have hip surgery and he wanted to do the stent first. His office called to tell me there was a mass on my right kidney. Karen took me to the Mayo Clinic in Rochester and in two weeks it was out. The cancer was contained to the one kidney, truly a miracle!

In January of 2011 the "lifesaver" doctor put the stent in and in May I finally had the right hip replaced. I had my last six month check in January of 2013 at the Mayo and am now two years cancer free!

Right now I'm in good shape and go back to the Mayo every six months for a checkup.

In May of 2012 we helped Uncle Nord celebrate his 100th Birthday! He is a great guy and doing quite well. He will be 101 in May! Onstads are Long Lived!

Celebrating Uncle Nord's 100th Birthday, 2012

Barb, me, Pete, Jeanne, and Nord

The lefse tradition continues!

Granddaughter Jansina helping make Lefse

My grandson, Jaymes, baking lefse

Trips

I've been in every state except Alaska. Now my travels are to Oconomowoc and Milwaukee, WI., Chicago, IL., and Fargo and Bismarck, ND. I'm glad I am still able to drive.

Sis, Ellie, Janette, and me on a trip to Seattle, WA in 1994

Hostfest in Minot, ND with Verna, 2000

Me, Verna, and Bill at Epcot in 2000

July 2012, visiting Margaret with Jeanne

Arizona with Jeanne, February 2013

I guess I'm not finished traveling yet. In March of 2013 I went on an enjoyable trip to Arizona, staying with Jeanne and Wayne in Green Valley for a week. It was nice to leave Minnesota snow and enjoy warmer weather and good company.

I also saw Pete and Marti there. They all spend a few months each winter in Green Valley, about thirty miles south of Tucson.

Back to my roots: The Onstad Township (where I was born) Town Hall

Hawaiian Cruise with my grandson, on our balcony

There's our ship!

Jaymes and I enjoying dinner on the ship's restaurant

Me and my grandson overlooking one of the islands

A Hawaiian waterfall

Enjoying Drinks on the deck

Enjoying the sun in Hawaii

In May 2013, my grandson Jaymes and I went on a Hawaiian cruise. We flew to Honolulu and cruised around, stopping at all the Hawaiian Islands. Jaymes was great to travel with, and we had a wonderful time in Hawaii. I still can't believe I did it!

Thank you to Jaymes for going with me, and to my granddaughter, Jansina, for putting this book all together.

Epilogue
2020

I have the best family ever. These are all the things that have happened since I wrote the book.

In 2016, I made it to the final state on my list, Alaska, on a cruise with my grandchildren.

We went on the Skagway Whitepass Summit Tour railroad on a vintage train.

So many great meals on the ship!

We had a beautiful room with a balcony in our cruise ship.

One of the many towel animals we were surprised with throughout the cruise.

On one of the last nights of the trip, we saw the Northern Lights!

The glass elevator in the ship.

Watching a glacier!

Our final stop was in Vancouver, where we visited the suspension bridge.

For my 90th birthday (2017), my family surprised me with a trip to Florida! I thought I was going to Chicago or someplace close, and they told me the morning of—giving me just enough time to pack clothes for a warmer climate.

We stayed in a suite with a kitchen, dining room, and living room.

Our suite's balcony was large enough for all five of us!

We visited Disney Springs while we were there.

My 91st birthday (2018) brought more surprises: Dinner with the Olsons and a surprise lunch with friends and neighbors.

In 2019, my 92nd birthday brought even more surprises!

My family took me to Crooner's for a country show and dinner—and a big surprise: Olsons and Weights again!

Jansina took me to see the Church Basement Ladies (the only show of theirs I hadn't yet seen), and Karen, Jansina, and I watched the Shen Yun Chinese dancers; beautiful!

Jaymes took me to lunch at the Gasthof German restaurant.

This year (2020) marks 9 years kidney cancer free. In 2018 I had three days of radiation to remove a small, cancerous legion on my lung.

I am truly blessed, and I mean every word of that.

2021 Update

 With the COVID-19 pandemic, I have been staying home since March 2020. Jaymes and Jansina have been working from home since then, and we have moved our weekly family nights to Zoom. Occasionally (Thanksgiving, Christmas, and most recently my 94th birthday) we will all quarantine for two weeks so we can safely see one another.

 Jaymes and Jansina have taken over lefse baking for good. In 2020, they made two batches—enough to share with family and a few friends.

 These past few years have also brought some surgeries. In August of 2017 I had a Watchman implanted in my heart; in November of 2020, a Pacemaker; and in December of 2020, an ablation. Finally, in January of 2021 I had an Abdominal Aortic Aneurysm repaired.

 Each time after I left the hospital and needed someone to stay overnight, Jansina was there to help.

 Karen has been my caregiver, taking me to doctor, clinic, and hospital appointments.

 I am forever grateful to all the Grossmans for all their help; I love them all!

Liz's Lefse

7 pounds of potatoes (approx.); add salt. Cook, do not overcook.

In large bowl drain and mash potatoes with:

5 Tbsp butter

4 Tbsp Crisco

1/8 Cup sugar

Small amount of milk, if needed. Will depend on how much moisture in the potatoes.

After mashing, rice and cool, usually overnight.

Add to riced potatoes about 2 to 2/12 cups flour, mix, then knead until not too sticky to roll out. Use an ice cream scoop to make balls of dough. Put on floured cookie sheet and refrigerate. Roll out on cloth covered, floured board with a sleeve covered lefse rolling pin until very thin.

Bake on grill, flip once and bake on other side. Place between cloths to cool.

My grandchildren and me baking lefse together

Scan for a lefse tutorial (Featuring the author!)

Not working? Type this link instead:

www.youtube.com/watch?v=V1MrtShvwHo

Rivershore Books

Website: www.rivershorebooks.com

Facebook: www.facebook.com/rivershore.books

Twitter: www.twitter.com/rivershorebooks

Email: info@rivershorebooks.com